ROBOTS AND ROBOTICS
High-risk Robots

Tony Hyland

A+

Smart Apple Media

This edition first published in 2008 in the United States of America by Smart Apple Media.

Smart Apple Media
2140 Howard Drive West
North Mankato, Minnesota 56003

First published in 2007 by
MACMILLAN EDUCATION AUSTRALIA PTY LTD
627 Chapel Street, South Yarra, Australia 3141

Visit our Web site at www.macmillan.com.au or go directly to www.macmillanlibrary.com.au

Associated companies and representatives throughout the world.

Library of Congress Cataloging-in-Publication Data

Hyland, Tony.
    High-risk robots / by Tony Hyland.
    p. cm. — (Robots and robotics)
    Includes index.
    ISBN 978-1-59920-119-1
    1. Manipulators (Mechanism)—Juvenile literature. 2. Robots, Industrial—Juvenile literature.
    3. Materials handling—Safety measures—Automatic control—Juvenile literature. 4. Extreme
    environments—Safety measures—Automatic control—Juvenile literature. I. Title. II. Series.

    T55.3.M35H53 2007
    629.8'92—dc22

                                                                                        2007004744

Edited by Margaret Maher
Text and cover design by Ivan Finnegan, iF Design
Page layout by Ivan Finnegan, iF Design
Photo research by Legend Images

Printed in U.S.

Acknowledgements
The author and the publisher are grateful to the following for permission to reproduce copyright material:

Front cover photograph: Talon robot in Baghdad, Iraq by US Army, Jonathan Montgomery.

Photos courtesy of:
Aquarius Collection, © Walt Disney, p. 17; © Hervé Collart/Sygma/Corbis, p. 18; CSIRO Australia, pp. 19, 25; DARPA, p. 21; Woods Hole
Oceanographic Institu/AFP/Getty Images, p. 16; Lockheed Martin photo, p. 23; © Duncan McLean, Vice President of Oceaneering, p. 14;
Prof. Giovanni Muscato, http://www.robotic.diees.unict.it, p. 13; NASA, p. 26; Bill Ingalls/NASA, p. 12; NASA/JPL, p. 27; NASA/JSC, p. 29;
NOAA, pp. 5, 15; OCRobotics, p. 11; Photolibrary/Adam Hart-Davis/Science Photo Library, p. 10; Photolibrary/Peter Menzel/Science Photo Library,
p. 28; US Air Force, Staff Sgt. Tony R. Tolley, p. 24; US Army, Sgt Lorie Jewell, p. 22; US Army, Jonathan Montgomery, p. 1; US Marines Corp,
Lance CPL M.L. Meier, p. 20; US Navy, 1st Class Robert R. McRill, pp. 6, 9; US Navy, 3rd Class Kenneth G. Takada, p. 7;
US Navy, 1st Class Jeremy L. Wood, pp. 4, 8.

Background textures courtesy of Photodisc.

Contents

Robots	**4**
Bomb disposal robots	**6**
Robotic emergency workers	**8**
Radiation-proof robots	**10**
Volcano explorers	**12**
Underwater robots	**14**
Mining robots	**18**
Robots at war	**20**
Flying robots	**24**
Robots in space	**26**
Future robots	**28**
Make a model rescue robot	**30**
Glossary	**31**
Index	**32**

GLOSSARY WORDS

When a word is printed in **bold**, you can look up its meaning in the glossary on page 31.

Bomb disposal robots

In some countries, terrorist bombs are a regular threat. Bombs can be in packages left in buildings, or in cars parked nearby. **Bomb disposal** experts often use robots make the bombs safe.

Danger: unexploded bomb!

During World War II, highly trained soldiers disarmed bombs. Many solders were killed or injured if the bombs exploded. Since then, bomb disposal experts have helped develop robots that can disarm bombs.

Remote control robots

Robots such as **Hobo** and **Talon** can be used to disable these bombs. These six-wheeled vehicles can roll into almost any area. The robots are **radio-controlled**, so that the operator can stay safely out of the way. They carry video cameras and tools that operators can use on the bombs.

The Talon 3B can go almost anywhere on its caterpillar tracks.

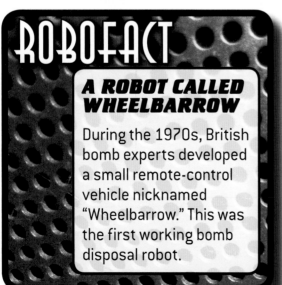

ROBOFACT

A ROBOT CALLED WHEELBARROW

During the 1970s, British bomb experts developed a small remote-control vehicle nicknamed "Wheelbarrow." This was the first working bomb disposal robot.

Modern bomb disposal robots have video cameras so the operator can watch what the robot is doing.

Dealing with bombs

Large, modern bomb disposal robots have many ways of dealing with a suspected bomb. The operator can watch through the robot's video cameras as the robot approaches the bomb. The robots also have gas and odor detectors. These can tell the operator what explosive is inside the bomb.

Andros F-6A

The most advanced bomb disposal robot today is the **Andros F-6A**. The robot's arm has a powerful rod that can smash car windows to get at bombs inside a car, and it carries a shotgun, which can blast open door locks. The robot's arm also holds a small water cannon, which will ruin the inner workings of most bombs. The Andros F-6A can be fitted with grippers and other tools to disarm bombs before they go off.

Robotic emergency workers

When buildings collapse or mines cave in, survivors are often trapped inside. Emergency workers come to the rescue, but their work is dangerous. Today, there are small robots that can go inside damaged buildings, looking for survivors.

Search and rescue

Search and rescue robots are similar to those used for bomb disposal. Often, they are made from the same base, but have different equipment and tools attached. They are usually on wheels or **caterpillar tracks**. These can roll easily over rough ground. Their main task is to go into dangerous areas and send video images to rescuers on the outside. Rescuers can see if anyone is trapped, and whether it is safe to enter the area.

The iRobot Packbot is a small robot that can be used for exploring dangerous areas.

Large and small rescuers

Search and rescue robots come in different sizes and shapes. The iRobot PackBot is small and light, but very strong. It can go into very small areas in collapsed buildings or tunnels. It sends back video and sound to the controllers.

The Talon robot, which is also used for bomb disposal, is much larger. It can be adapted for searching for survivors, with video cameras and gas detectors.

Researchers are developing a robotic ambulance for use in disaster areas or battle zones. It will be able to find survivors, load them on board, and take them to a safe area.

Rescue robot competitions

Making a robot that is intelligent enough to search for survivors is a real challenge. Every year, students at schools and universities around the world enter competitions to make the best rescuers. The robots have to search a set-up area, find a "survivor," and pull the survivor to safety.

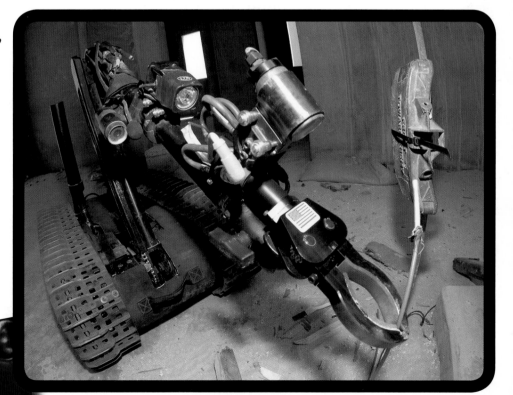

The Talon robot can be equipped with video cameras and other sensing equipment.

Radiation-proof robots

In many countries, **nuclear reactors** are used to generate electricity. The **radiation** from nuclear reactors is deadly to humans. Robots are sometimes used in areas where humans cannot go.

Rescue robots

There are several important jobs for robots in nuclear power plants. One robot that workers hope will never be needed is the rescue robot. This robot could rescue workers injured in a nuclear accident.

A designer makes adjustments to Robug.

Robug is an eight-legged rescue robot that looks like a large crab or spider. It is strong enough to climb into a damaged building and drag out an injured human. The robot can be fitted with lights, cameras, and radiation detectors. These help controllers direct it.

ROBOFACT

NUCLEAR DISASTER RESCUE ROBOTS

In 1986, the reactor at a nuclear power station exploded at Chernobyl in Ukraine. Nearly 50 workers died from radiation poisoning. Today, new radiation-proof rescue robots are being developed. These robots could save workers in future nuclear disasters.

Repairs and maintenance

The radiation inside a nuclear reactor can kill humans very quickly. Normally, the radioactive area is completely shielded. In areas that are not protected, robots do all repairs and **maintenance**. Most of the work consists of cleaning and repairing pipes that contain hot steam.

One-armed robots

Many robots used in nuclear reactors look like the one-armed robots that work in car factories. They have a large, single arm fitted with grippers and other tools for their job. Some, such as the Japanese RaBOT, move on caterpillar tracks like a tank. Others move along a rail.

Pipe-cleaning robots

When a problem developed inside pipes at a Swedish nuclear reactor, the OCRobotics Snake-arm robot repaired the damage. This robot has a long, flexible arm that can reach right inside the pipes. Some reactors use a small robot for cleaning. It rolls along inside the pipes, cleaning as it goes.

The Snake-arm robot can reach deep into pipes to repair them.

Volcano explorers

Scientists who study volcanoes go into very dangerous territory, deep inside volcanic craters. Today, robots have been designed to do this job.

Exploring craters

Robots that go inside a volcanic crater must travel over very rocky, hot ground. They are out of the range of radio controllers, so they must move around without help from humans.

A robot named Dante II was used to explore Mount Spurr in Alaska in 1994. It worked for a while, but its eight legs were not stable. It fell over and had to be rescued. A later robot, named Robovolc, was designed with six wheels. The wheels keep it stable as it explores.

ROBOFACT

A MARS ROVER EXPLORES EARTH

The Russian robot Marsokhod Lama was designed to work on Mars. Instead, it has been used to explore volcanoes and deserts on Earth. Its mapping skills and specially designed wheels make it perfect for this job.

Dante II was used to explore the crater of an active volcano.

Up Close

ROBOT
Robovolc

JOB
Gathering gas, rock, and lava samples

MAKER
University of Catania, Sicily

SKILLS
Traveling over rough, rocky ground, collecting samples in volcanic areas

GUIDANCE SYSTEM
GPS satellite navigation

SIZE
30 inches (76 cm) long,
24 inches (61 cm) wide,
24 inches (61 cm) high

Robovolc can drive up a volcano's side and then into the crater. It can collect samples and data in places that are not safe for humans. Robovolc's six independent wheels keep it rolling over the rockiest ground. Each wheel has its own motor. If any wheel becomes stuck, the others will keep Robovolc going.

Professor Giovanni Muscato and his students at the University of Catania built Robovolc. They use it to explore Mt. Etna, an active volcano in Sicily. Robovolc can collect samples of poisonous volcanic gas. It can also pick up rock and lava samples.

Underwater robots

The world far underwater is dangerous for humans. It is cold and airless. Robots are ideal for exploring the deep oceans.

Remotely operated vehicles

Most underwater robots are remotely operated vehicles (ROVs). These machines can dive in deep water. They are controlled through a long cable, while their operators stay on the surface.

ROVs range from tiny vehicles weighing less than 7 pounds (3 kg), to huge machines weighing more than 4 tons. Some carry video cameras. The largest have robotic arms for working underwater.

Autonomous underwater vehicles

Autonomous underwater vehicles (AUVs) follow their own program, guiding themselves through the sea. They are used for mapping the seafloor, as well as for taking scientific measurements.

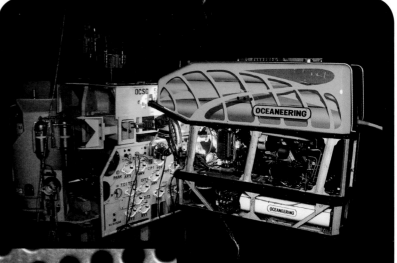

An ROV can work deep under the ocean.

ROBOFACT

UNDERWATER GLIDER

A new type of AUV, known as a Seaglider, can travel for weeks under the sea. It looks like a small jet plane. Its wings keep it steady in the water.

Who uses underwater robots?

There are many different reasons for using underwater robots. They are used by oil companies, marine biologists, and marine archeologists.

Oil companies

Oil companies set up huge **drilling platforms** in the sea. Divers do some of the maintenance work underneath the drilling platform. Large ROVs can dive far deeper than humans, to work in deep water. Operators can inspect the platform using the ROV's video cameras, and repair it using the ROV's built-in tools.

Marine biologists

Marine biologists study the living creatures of the sea. Many unusual creatures live deep in the ocean, where only ROVs can travel. Biologists using ROVs have discovered many creatures that no one has ever seen before.

Marine archeologists

Marine archeologists study ancient shipwrecks. They use ROVs to look closely at ships that have sunk in deep water. ROVs can also collect ancient objects, such as tools and coins, from these ships.

Some ROVs are used to collect samples of plants from the sea.

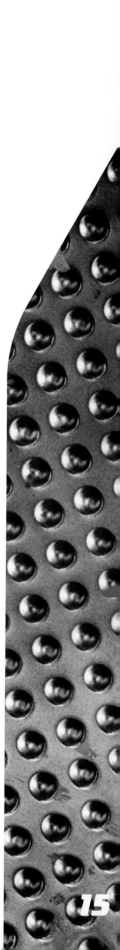

The wreck of the Titanic

In 1912, the *Titanic* sank in the middle of the Atlantic Ocean. Explorer Robert Ballard discovered the wreck in 1985, using robotic underwater vehicles.

Exploring the *Titanic*

Ballard's ship stopped on the ocean surface, directly above the wreck. A small crew traveled down to the *Titanic* in a **submarine**. From the submarine, the crew controlled an ROV called Jason Junior which could fit through small openings inside the *Titanic*.

Jake and Elwood were sent to explore the *Titanic*.

James Cameron's expedition

James Cameron directed the 1997 movie *Titanic*. In 2001, he sent an expedition to film a documentary about the wreck of the *Titanic*, called *Ghosts of the Abyss*. Cameron's expedition used two submarines with robotic arms. Each submarine carried a small ROV. The two ROVs, nicknamed Jake and Elwood, explored inside the *Titanic*.

ROBOFACT

LEAVE IT ALONE

Robert Ballard believed that no one should take things from the *Titanic*. Other explorers have gone down with ROVs and collected items such as tools and bags.

Up Close

ROBOTS
Jake and Elwood

JOB
Exploring inside sunken ships

MAKER
Mike Cameron
(James Cameron's brother), U.S.

SKILLS
Entering confined spaces,
shooting video images

SIZE
28 inches (71 cm) long,
16 inches (40 cm) wide,
16 inches (40 cm) high

WEIGHT
77 pounds (35 kg)

Jake and Elwood were specially built for *Ghosts of the Abyss*. They carried lights, video cameras, and batteries. Each was attached to one of the two submarines by a 2,000-foot (600 m) **fiber-optic cable**.

Jake and Elwood were small enough to enter the rooms and cabins of the *Titanic*. They sent video images back to the submarines through the fiber-optic cable. Controllers in each submarine directed the ROVs toward the most interesting places.

Once, Elwood's batteries ran out of power inside the *Titanic*. The controllers used Jake to drag Elwood to safety.

James Cameron used Jake and Elwood again to explore the sunken German battleship *Bismarck* in 2002.

Mining robots

Underground mining is a dangerous job. Miners can be killed or injured if mines collapse. Today, robots do some of this dangerous work.

Robotic cutters

Most mining is done with large earth-cutting machines, controlled by miners. Researchers are developing robotic systems to control these machines. This will allow the miners to stay away from the dust and noise of the cutting area.

Australian mining robots

Researchers in Australia have developed many of the world's mining robots. They have made automatic loaders to collect and load coal. There are even robotic mine trucks that follow tracks inside the mine, carrying loads of coal to the surface.

A robotic coal mining machine can cut tons of coal very quickly.

ROBOFACT

CAVE CRAWLER

Many mines have old tunnels that have never been properly mapped. These could be dangerous if miners accidentally dig into them. Cave Crawler is a robot that can roll along inside old mines. It uses **radar** to create an exact map of the area.

Up Close

ROBOT
Automatic **dragline**

JOB
Mining in **open-cut mines**

MAKER
Commonwealth Scientific and
Industrial Research Organisation,
Australia

SKILLS
Digging coal,
keeping accurate maps of the
mining area

SIZE
245 feet (75 m) tall,
330 feet (100 m) long

WEIGHT
3,500 tons

The world's largest robot is a huge coal shovel. It works on an open-cut mine
in northeastern Australia.

The robot drags an enormous shovel across the surface of the mine,
collecting coal. It has sensors that tell it exactly how much coal it is carrying.
When the bucket is full, the machine empties the coal at a dump point. Then,
it swings back to start collecting more coal.

As the dragline moves along, its robotic sensors build an accurate map of the
mine. The robot uses this map to decide where to work next.

Robots at war

Modern warfare is more dangerous than ever before. New weapons can hit targets from a distance. Robotic machines are already used in warfare, often as **scouts**.

Scouting robots

Small, tough robots such as PackBot and Talon are useful as scouts. They carry video cameras and sensors that can detect gas or explosives. They search inside caves and tunnels before soldiers go in.

Big Dog

Larger robots are useful for carrying equipment. Big Dog is a four-legged robot about the size of a mule. It can walk or run across rocky ground without losing its balance, carrying packs and ammunition.

ROBOFACT

TOUGH ROBOTS

Combat robots must be very strong. One Talon robot was blown off a bridge into a river in Iraq. The controller was able to drive the robot along the riverbed underwater, and out onto the riverbank. After a few minor repairs it was soon back at work.

Big Dog robots can run quickly in any direction without falling over.

Large robotic vehicles

Large vehicles such as trucks and ambulances can also be turned into robots. Such robotic vehicles could bring supplies to soldiers and carry away wounded people.

DARPA Challenge

The DARPA Challenge is a competition for teams to build a robotic car or truck. The vehicle must travel across more than 120 miles of desert without human help. In 2004, the first year of the competition, no vehicle completed the course. Most crashed or simply got lost.

In 2005, five teams completed the race. The winning vehicle crossed the desert in just under seven hours. It followed its built-in guidance system to avoid rocks and bushes.

Future vehicles

Once it has been proven that the robotic system will work, it can be built into many large vehicles. One estimate is that by 2015, one-third of the trucks and other vehicles used by the United States army will be robotic.

A robotic car named Stanley was the winner of the DARPA Challenge in 2005.

Robotic weapons for soldiers

Most of the robots currently used by the military provide support for soldiers. They disarm bombs, search buildings, or carry equipment. It is possible to fit weapons to robots such as Talon. However, the robots cannot use weapons without human guidance. They do not have enough intelligence to tell an enemy soldier from any other human.

Turning weapons into robots

Many large weapons, such as missiles and **artillery**, could be turned into robots. They would just need computer sensors and controllers. Robotic artillery and missiles would still need humans controlling them. However, they could more accurately zero in on their targets.

ROBOFACT

CAN ROBOTS REALLY GO TO WAR?

Today's robots could not go to war by themselves. They are not intelligent enough to know what human beings are. They would not be able to fight without a human directing them.

This Talon robot has been fitted with machine guns as well as cameras.

ROBOT
Loitering attack
missile (LAM)

JOB
Search for enemy
targets,
then attack them

MAKER
Lockheed Martin,
U.S.

SKILLS
Flying,
radar and video
searching

SIZE
5 feet (1.5 m) long

WEIGHT
110 pounds (50kg)

The LAM is known as a hunter-killer missile. It is a small missile that can fly back and forth looking for enemy targets. This activity is called loitering.

The LAM has a small, powerful engine and large wings. It can fly for about 30 minutes, searching for targets. It sends radar and video images back to its controllers. Once the controllers select a target from the radar and video data, the robot aims itself at the target and flies down to attack. The missile explodes when it hits the target.

Armed forces have used missiles for many years, but LAM is the first truly robotic missile.

Flying robots

Robotic airplanes and helicopters can fly in dangerous areas, such as over battlefields or forest fires. Some are full size machines, while others are tiny.

Radio-controlled planes and helicopters have been used for many years. They must be controlled by a human operator or they will crash. Flying robots are called unmanned aerial vehicles (UAVs). They use information from sensors to control their own flight. They can adjust their flight in bad weather, and land by themselves if their fuel is running low.

UAVs at war

UAVs can be used during wars. These machines can fly over enemy locations. They send back pictures of troop movements and hidden forces. Some UAVs can be fitted with missiles to attack enemies.

ROBOFACT

UNMANNED FIGHTER JETS

Robotic fighter jets perform like piloted jets. They can attack other planes, or troops on the ground. They can work out their own attack and defense plans without human help.

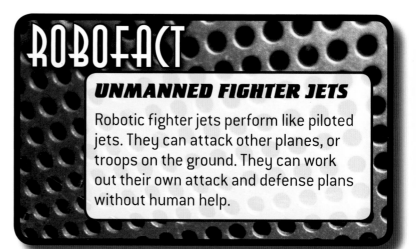

The Predator UAV can be used to spy on enemies or carry missiles.

Peaceful uses for UAVs

UAVs have many uses away from war zones. Robotic planes can collect weather and mapping data. They can use cameras and other equipment to collect useful information.

Small robotic helicopters could be useful in fires and other disasters. They could fly above the area, sending back images to emergency workers on the ground. Robotic helicopters can even inspect power lines, checking for faults.

Independent UAVs

Researchers are working on ways to make UAVs more independent. A UAV computer needs to control many things at once. It controls the robot's height, speed, and direction, while also carrying out its main job.

Scientists working on UAVs compete in the International Aerial Robotics Competition. Their small UAVs must complete several difficult tasks. They must find a particular building, fly through the window, take photos, and then leave. So far, no UAV has been able to finish this task.

A small robotic helicopter can send video images to emergency workers.

Robots in space

Humans have only just begun to explore space. Only a few astronauts have landed on the Moon. Robots can go far beyond the Moon, to places that humans will never reach.

Satellites and probes

The first spacecraft were **satellites**, such as *Sputnik 1*, which was launched in 1957. Within a few years, probes were sent to the Moon. In 1970, a probe traveled as far as Venus.

Modern probes and satellites are robotic vehicles. Their onboard computers control most of their actions. Probes such as *Galileo* and *Cassini* have traveled past the planets, sending back amazing new data and photos.

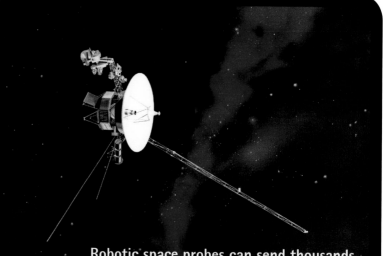

Robotic space probes can send thousands of images back to Earth for scientists.

ROBOFACT

COMET LANDER

In 2005, the probe *Deep Impact* reached the comet Tempel 1. It launched a smaller probe that crashed onto the comet's surface. *Deep Impact* sent pictures and other data back to researchers on Earth. It was the first time a probe had ever come into contact with a comet.

Rovers, such as *Mars Science Lab*, give us a close-up look at other planets.

Exploring the surface

Many probes have been sent to land on the surface of the Moon and the planets. Probably the most successful early probes were *Viking 1* and *Viking 2*. These landed on Mars in 1976. They sent back the first close-up photos of the surface of Mars. They also conducted experiments to see if life could exist in Martian soil.

Rovers

Rovers do not have to stay in one spot. They can explore a large area. In 2004, two rovers called *Spirit* and *Opportunity* were sent to Mars. They were expected to work for three months. Instead, they spent over two years examining the rocks and soil of Mars.

Future exploration

Rovers have been so successful that more are being designed. A huge rover called *Mars Science Lab* will land on Mars in 2008. Other rovers will probably explore the moons of Jupiter and Saturn in years to come.

Future robots

Robots are becoming smarter and better equipped every year. Will they ever completely take the place of humans in dangerous jobs?

Preventing deaths and injuries

The jobs today with the highest rates of death and injury are logging, commercial fishing, and truck driving. Robots of the future could work in these jobs, helping to prevent injury to humans.

Developing smarter and stronger robots

Many of the robots operating today are still very limited. Search and rescue robots are useful for searching dangerous areas. However, none can give first aid to victims, or pull survivors from rubble. Researchers are trying to develop robots that can do this.

Automated guided vehicles (AGVs) are robotic trucks that can move around without a human driver. So far, AGVs only work in limited places, such as mines and docks. Researchers predict that eventually AGVs will be intelligent enough to drive on major public roads.

Researchers are building new robots, such as this crab robot, to do dangerous jobs.

Robots must be tested and programmed to cooperate before they travel to the Moon or Mars.

Future robotic space explorers

Robots will continue to be essential in space exploration. Human astronauts will return to the Moon by 2015. They will go to Mars by 2020. However, robots will go first.

Robots working together

Crews of robots will be sent to the Moon and Mars to set up base camps before humans arrive. The robots will need to work together, carrying and assembling sections of the base. This will take more intelligent cooperation than any robots are able to achieve now.

Exploring the solar system

Future plans include a highly intelligent probe that will travel to Jupiter's moons in 2015. It will orbit Jupiter's moons for about a year each. Other robotic probes will head to the other major planets.

NASA is also researching underwater ROVs, such as the Seaglider. Advanced ROVs will explore the oceans of Jupiter's moons. They will send data back to Earth.

Make a model rescue robot

If you have access to a Lego Mindstorms kit, you can create a rescue robot suitable for the Robocup Junior competition. Robocup Junior is a competition for elementary and high school students. Teams of students build robots to compete.

There are three sections in Robocup Junior: Robot Soccer, Robot Rescue, and Robot Dance. In the Robot Rescue section, robots have to follow a track and search through an area to find a "survivor."

The top teams compete in world championships, held in a different country every year. You can find out more through the Robocup Junior Web site.

What you need

- Lego Mindstorms programming brick
- Lego Technics pieces or other model pieces that will fit
- computer and software to program the robot

What to do

1. Prepare your model with the brick as the centerpiece.
2. Include two axles and four wheels.
3. Include an arm.
4. Program the robot to roll forward.
5. Program the robot to stop and turn back when it hits a white line.

Work with friends or classmates to build a robot that can compete in the Robocup Junior program.

Have fun!

Glossary

Andros F-6A - a powerful robotic vehicle that can be equipped for many different missions

artillery - large transportable guns, such as cannons

autonomous underwater vehicles - robotic vehicles that can operate underwater without human control

bomb disposal - disarming and removing bombs

caterpillar tracks - large tracks used on tanks, bulldozers and robots so they can travel across rough ground

disarm - to make an unexploded bomb safe

dragline - a huge coal-mining crane

drilling platforms - large platforms holding oil-drilling crews and equipment

fibre-optic cable - a cable made of very thin glass fibres, used for transmitting data

GPS satellite navigation - locating an exact position using data sent from satellites

Hobo - a small robotic vehicle used for bomb disposal

maintenance - repair and replacement of damaged parts

nuclear reactors - machines which contain and control nuclear energy

open-cut mines - mines where miners dig an open pit, instead of tunnelling under the surface

program - to install the instructions that control a robot's actions

radar - a system that uses radio waves to detect objects in the surrounding area

radiation - rays of energy, which can be harmful to humans

radio-controlled - controlled by signals sent as radio waves

rovers - robots designed to explore the surface of another planet

satellites - objects in orbit around a planet or other body in space

science fiction - stories based on futuristic scientific ideas

scouts - people or robots that go ahead of everyone else to look for signs of danger

space probes - unmanned space vehicles that collect data about other planets

submarine - a vehicle designed to operate underwater

surgical robots - robots capable of performing surgical operations

Talon - a medium-sized robotic vehicle that can be equipped for bomb disposal or other missions

Index

A

ambulances   9, 21
Andros F-6A   7
artillery   22
automated guided vehicles
    (AVGs)   28
automatic draglines   19
autonomous underwater
    vehicles (AUVs)   14

B

Ballard, Robert   16
Big Dog   20

C

Cameron, James   16, 17
Cassini   26
caterpillar tracks   8, 11
Cave Crawler   18
coal mining   19
combat robots   20

D

Dante II   12
DARPA Challenge   21
Deep Impact   26

G

Galileo   26
Ghosts of the Abyss   16, 17

H

Hobo   6

I

International Aerial
    Robotics Competition   25
Iraq   20

J

Jake and Elwood   16, 17
Jason Junior   16

L

Lego   30
loitering attack missiles
    (LAMs)   23

M

marine archeologists   15
marine biologists   15
Mars   4, 12, 27, 29
Mars Science Lab   27
Marsokhod Lama   12
missiles   22, 23, 24
Moon   26, 27, 29
Mount Etna, Sicily   13
Mount Spurr, Alaska   12

N

nuclear reactors   10, 11

O

ocean expolartion   4, 5, 14,
    15, 16, 17
oil drilling   15
open-cut mining   19
Opportunity   27

P

PackBot   8, 9, 20
Predator UAV   24
programming   4, 30

R

RaBOT   11
radar   18, 23
radio-controlled robots   6, 24
rescue robots   5, 8, 9, 10, 22,
    28
remotely operated vehicles
    (ROVs)   14, 15, 16, 17, 29
Robocup Junior   30
robotic vehicles   18, 21, 26,
    27, 28
robotic weapons   22, 23
Robovolc   12, 13
Robug   10
rovers   27

S

scout robots   20
Seaglider   14, 29
sensors   19, 22, 24
Snake-arm robot   11
snakebots   8
space probes   5, 26, 27, 29
Spirit   27
Sputnik 1   26
submarines   16, 17

T

Talon   6, 9, 20, 22
Titanic   16, 17

U

unmanned aerial vehicles
    (UAVs)   24–5

W

Wheelbarrow   6